Finding the Lost Art of Family Storytelling

A Guide for Parents, Grandparents, and Family Historians

Joseph P. Jekot, M.Ed.

• Chicago •

Finding the Lost Art of Family Storytelling
A Guide for Parents, Grandparents, and Family Historians

Joseph P. Jekot, M.Ed.
Artwork and Illustrations by Linda Chlimoun

Published by
Joshua Tree Publishing
• Chicago •
JoshuaTreePublishing.com

All rights reserved. No part of this book may be reproduced or transmitted in any form or by any means, electronic or mechanical, including information storage and retrieval system without written permission from the publisher, except by a reviewer who may quote brief passages in a review.

13-Digit ISBN: 978-1-941049-57-0
Copyright © 2019 Joseph P. Jekot. All Rights Reserved.

Front Cover Image ©okalinichenko
Back Cover Image ©Tony Baggett

All Bible References:
Holy Bible, New International Version®, NIV® Copyright © 1973, 1978, 1984, 2011 by Biblica, Inc.® Used by permission. All rights reserved worldwide.

Disclaimer:
This book is designed to provide information about the subject matter covered. The opinions and information expressed in this book are those of the author, not the publisher. Every effort has been made to make this book as complete and as accurate as possible. However, there may be mistakes both typographical and in content. Therefore, this text should be used only as a general guide and not as the ultimate source of information. The author and publisher of this book shall have neither liability nor responsibility to any person or entity with respect to any loss or damage caused or alleged to be caused directly or indirectly by the information contained in this book.

Printed in the United States of America

For Maya,

You filled my world with endless stories . . .

Table of Contents

*****A Note to the Reader***** 6
Naked Truth and Parable 7
Introduction 9
In the Beginning 11
Sarah's Heart 13
The Big Picture 15
Creating the Big Picture 17
Making the Pictures Talk: Learning and Remembering Stories 25
Telling Stories in Ways that Inspire, Sing and Dance 31
Why Stories Touch the Soul 37
Bringing Meaning to Your Stories 43
Going from a Simple Story to a Complete Saga 47
An Application of the Longer Story 51
Learning How to Perform the Longer Story 53
The Greatest Stories Never Told 55
How to Record and Perform the Story of an Elder 57
Identifying the Overall Story 59
Starting and Maintaining a Family Storytelling Tradition 61
Parenting Through Story 65
Conclusion 71
Bibliography 75
Resources 77

*****A Note to the Reader*****

In writing this text, I have made it my practice to alternate between the feminine and masculine characters. Studies have shown that in reading references to gender in a text, the use of only one gender has a negative effect on the opposite gender. I chose to still use reference to gender because writing the text as gender free is very clumsy and makes reading the text awkward.

Naked Truth and Parable

Naked Truth walked down the street one day.
People turned their eyes away.

Parable arrived, draped in decoration.
People greeted Parable with celebration.

Naked Truth sat alone, sad and unattired.
"Why are you so miserable?" Parable inquired.

Naked Truth replied, "I'm not welcome anymore.
No one wants to see me. They chase me from their door."

"It is hard to look at Naked Truth," Parable explained.
"Let me dress you up a bit. Your welcome will be gained."

Parable dressed Naked Truth in story's fine attire,
with metaphor, poignant prose, and plots to inspire.

With laughter and tears and adventures to unveil,
together they went forth to spin a tale.

People opened their doors and served them their best
Naked Truth dressed in story was a welcome guest.

—a poem written by Heather Forest based on a tale told in Eastern Europe by the Maggid of Dubno, and eighteenth-century Hasidic rabbi. (Used with permission)

Introduction

Jay O'Callahan is presently one of the most celebrated professional storytellers in the country and possibly the world. He is universally known for his ability to weave wonderful tales from the most ordinary and common events and turn the simplest of characters into dastardly villains and valiant heroes. When asked how he does it, he simply responds, "Life is lived in the narrative, wherever you find life you will find story." Taking these words to heart has changed me as a minister, a teacher, and a father.

Story is the universal language of life. Communicating through the language of story allows me to relate to those around me in a personal and meaningful way. It also enhances the humor of my interactions with others. Being a high school teacher, I often ask my students this question, "Which activity brings you more pleasure, going to the homecoming dance or sharing the stories of going to the homecoming dance at the lunch table on Monday morning?" Inevitably, the answer is always sharing the stories on the following Monday. Why? Because, whether you are a parent, a teacher, or a minister, telling the stories of life is the act of reliving and celebrating it at the same moment.

Every human being was born to hear and tell stories, and in doing so, create and pass on those stories with spiritual messages to future generations. Stories are the language that speaks directly to the soul. They inspire and heal. The gift of story is the bridge between mortality and eternity. Celebrating life through story is a magic that makes us an image of God. For God is the greatest storyteller of all.

In the Beginning

In the beginning was the Word, and the word was with God,
and the Word was God. (John 1:1)

And the Word became flesh (John 1:14)

The basic tools for stories are words. It is through the power of words that great men and women have defined the principles which govern the dynamics of life, and they have used these words to harness and control nature. In the modern day, the goal of learning words is power.

However, it is the master storyteller who not only knows the power of words, but also the stories from which they came. Knowing the stories behind the words brings with it something that power can never control—mystery and wonder. As a classroom teacher for the past twenty-eight years, I have noticed that all the students really want are the answers to the tests. A recent survey concluded that the number of students who simply do not like school has risen eighty-five percent since 1980. I believe this is true. They are only focused on the words that will enhance their grade point average and raise their S.A.T. scores. Young people are not experiencing the wonder which comes with learning words. They do not see how words form a tapestry of history, knowledge, and human expression. They are not being mentored to weave all their knowledge into a story that gives life meaning. I believe that they are quickly becoming a story-less generation.

Let's examine the origin and meaning of the word **"word"** as it is referred to in the Biblical quote above. What does the word "Word", with the capital W, really mean? What are the words behind the word that makes it what is (in the example listed above, it is represented as something Divine). Looking directly at the phrase, "And the Word was God," means that a Word can be equated to God. And what is the story behind that?

To unify the terms Word and God, is to create the word Theology. When you take the word theology into syllables, you come up with the root "Theo" and the suffix "ology." Breaking the word into its meaning seems easy enough. The term "Theo" means God and the suffix "ology" means the study of something, which in this example would be the study of God. This is true, but the original word for "ology" was a Greek word. In its original form, the term is written as "logos." Most teachers and students stop at this point and say, "Well, it's all Greek to me." What they fail to realize is that this is only the beginning of the word's meaning.

In its original Greek form, the term "logos" was not a singular specific word which only meant "word"; it was a generic term that has a variety of meanings. The first way in which the term "logos" is translated is as the term story. Go back and reread the Gospel quote from above and use the term" story" wherever you see the term "Word." It has a very different meaning in that context. When taken in the context that it is written, it can also be interpreted as the meaning of, or the reckoning (awakening) of a truth. Another interpretation for the term is identity. All of us wear t-shirts or dress shirts with logos on them. A logo on a shirt gives that shirt a special meaning or an identity. It's not just any old shirt. It's a Polo shirt or an Izod shirt, and that gives the person who is wearing it a distinct identity. When written as "logoi," the term refers to a trance like state of consciousness associated with bliss. Yes, just like when we hear good poetry, the original purpose of words had the power to place the listener in a state of bliss.

Now let's put the term "Logos," as it is used in the Scripture statement above, in its complete context. Theology is the study of; the truth of; the meaning of; the words of; the story of; the reckoning of; the identity of; God. And the end result of hearing the words elevates the listener into a state of bliss. This certainly creates a much more powerful image than translating the "Word," as simply word. Words are wondrous things, and when placed into the context of a story, bring life to the Truth.

Sarah's Heart

Once upon a time there was a little girl named Sarah. She was so happy! She was so happy because her grandmother had just given her a brand-new doll as a gift. She held, hugged, and carried that doll throughout her grandma's house skipping and smiling with joy. She sat down in her grandmother's living room chair when she noticed something on the coffee table. It was a wool piece of cloth that was in the shape of a bright red heart. She thought that this would be the perfect cape for her doll.

It was a sunny day so Sarah's mother told her to go out and play while she talked to grandma. Sarah ran down the back stoop to the park down the block. When she came back, she had her doll but not the wool heart. Her mother said it was time to go before she realized the red heart was missing.

Through her tears she told her mother that she had taken the heart and it was now missing. Together they looked high and low. They searched every place they could possibly go, but to no avail. The heart was lost, and Sarah's mother angrily reminded her that she was told not to touch other people's things. She would have to tell her grandmother what happened.

Sarah's grandmother was sitting in her chair when Sarah entered the room. She was crying so hard she hyperventilated. Her grandmother picked Sarah up and placed her on her lap trying to calm the child. Finally, Sarah was able to communicate that she had taken the wool heart and lost it. Sarah's grandmother looked at the table and saw that it was gone. And then she said . . .

"Now calm yourself, my child. The heart is not lost. Let me tell you the story of that heart . . . On the day that I was born, my father was so proud and so happy that he went out and bought the biggest, the warmest, most beautiful blanket he could find. It was a glorious blanket and embroidered on it were the moon and the stars. In the very center of it was this little red heart.

"On the first day of my life, my father wrapped me in that blanket. It was so big I looked like a queen wearing a royal robe. I learned how to crawl on that blanket and took my first steps into the world right off of it. We used that blanket for our family picnics for years. Sitting on it underneath the shade of the tall trees during the day and gazing on the stars at night.

"As the years moved on, the material began to get old so my mother put the blanket away. When I was a young woman, I found it and was so in love with it that I made it into a wool skirt. I was wearing the skirt the night I met your grandfather. But soon, the material on the bottom began to fall apart so I took it and sewed it into a sweater. I was wearing that sweater on the chilly night your grandfather first kissed me and told me he loved me.

"Now we were married, and I wanted to wear that sweater so much that the wool in the elbows wore out. So, I cut and I snipped, and I sewed it into a shawl. I was wearing that shawl the night I told your grandfather that I was going to have a baby—your mother.

"Finally, the shawl became so worn down that the only part left was the little heart from the center. The moon and the stars seemed to have faded away. But they hadn't really faded away for they are so much still in my heart and my world. You see Sarah; the heart is not gone because its story is still in my heart. And now the story is in your heart as well."

And grandma pointed at Sarah and tickled her watching that beautiful smile return to her face.

The Big Picture

"Your old men will dream dreams,
your young men will see visions." (Joel 2:28)

When fully engaged in the activity of storytelling, the teller assumes the role of a medium that uses words to connect the listener's souls to the infinite wonders of life. As important as words are, in the art of storytelling, words are used only as tools, a means to an end—not the end in and of itself. Words create pictures, and the pictures are the source of visions. The irony of seeing the big picture of life is that it can only truly be seen when processed through the unique imagination of each individual. No two people relate to God in the exact same way. No two people walk the exact same path in life to searching for meaning and truth. When I perform a story, which touches the souls of my listeners, no two people hear the same story. When they go home to tell the story to the people in their lives, no two people tell the same story.

The biggest detriment to communicating lessons and the meaning of life to the children of this generation is their inability and lack of desire to use their imaginations. The storyteller is a medium who uses words to translate images (visions) from inside her spirit to the spirits of her listeners. When people are constantly watching television, or what my mother used to affectionately call "The Idiot Box," the pictures are already given to the viewer, so she does not have to create her own. Modern day video games have added to the problem, but it is the music video which has exacerbated it.

If you watch the news each night, you will notice that the camera angle filming the newscaster is changed every eight seconds. Two newscasters go back and forth sharing stories. The purpose of this is to hold the viewers' attention. It is to keep the mind from wandering. Sit down and watch a music video and you will notice that, not only does the camera angle of the singer change, but the entire scene including background, changes every two seconds. This constant stimulation and immediate gratification produce its ill effects in the fact that many young people do not want to read books anymore. Reading a book used to be a very rewarding activity in which the reader could actively create their own images. Reading challenges a person to go into his own imagination and create his own images of what is being read. People are losing, or forfeiting, the creative ability to create their own unique images of the world. They are not dreaming their own dreams and seeing their own visions. They are losing the Big Picture. In learning how to tell even the most simple of stories, this problem can be reversed.

A person will always choose a live performance over a video version of it. Give any young person the choice of watching Jessica Simpson on the television, or actually going to her live concert. The person will always choose going to the live concert. One of the biggest assets to the storyteller is that she performs live. At any moment in the story, something spontaneous can happen. This draws the audience and teller together in a way that is not possible with videos. Someone may comment on one of the story's characters in a funny way. The narrator may assume the role of several different characters of a personal story that the members in the audience already know. A member from that audience may add to the impression of the character that the teller has already developed, making it more fun for all the listeners. A variety of things can flow from a story that a listener could never get from watching the television. Telling stories is a communal activity that is very personal at the same time. It challenges listeners to use their imaginations and to dream their own dreams.

Creating the Big Picture

Telling a Simple Story

Even though socially conditioned attention deficit disorders have hampered the imagination of the present generation, I believe that a simple verbal story still continues to be the most powerful activity of learning and entertainment. Why? There are two reasons. The first is that a well-told story touches the soul of the listener. The feeling that comes from not just listening to, but experiencing a story is more than just cathartic. It does more than produce an emotional release—it creates a fire in the soul of the listener. The second is that any story can be told by creating four simple images in the imagination of the listener. Even the shortest of stories can have the most powerful effect.

When you drive a car down the road, you start out by giving your complete attention to what is going on outside the car, and to the rules of the road. Before too long, you are driving the car, but your mind is somewhere else. In your imagination, you start thinking about whatever is going on in your life outside the car. It's as if you are operating the car using a psychological auto pilot. You are daydreaming, and when you daydream, you daydream in the language of story. The activity of driving the car is your consciousness moving in the real world on a straight line. There aren't any crazy characters and passionate climaxes in your thoughts as you operate the car. Your consciousness is simply going from point A to B. However, when you daydream, there are characters, problems, and climaxes racing through your thoughts.

If you analyze the literal context and themes of your daydreams, you will realize that they are not just isolated random thoughts—but stories. I believe each day dream can only be one of four types of stories or dramas. These include romance, comedy, tragedy, and the western or the hero drama. Our minds are constantly going in and out of a daydreaming or a dreaming state.

When you daydream, do you think about your love relationships (Romance)?

Are you remembering a funny joke that someone told you? Do you fantasize about how funny it would be if your boss fell off the chair from which he pontificates, and had to go home with a sore back (Comedy)?

Are you filled with sorrow while daydreaming of someone you love not living a happy life? Do you think about your inability to overcome some of your own misfortunes (Tragedy)?

How often, when you daydream, is your mind ablaze with strategies and interventions that would help you save the day and become a Hero (Western) for yourself or those around you?

A circular thought process occurs, whereby you identify a problem and think of it in terms of a Romance, Tragedy, Comedy, or Western. Soon images with strong emotions dramatize the story in your mind. Next you identify with the major character of your dramas. In the case of the Western, you become the hero of the story. Finally, you begin to see the main character as a transformed person. The psychic energy and images produced from this character become the blueprint of how you are going to live your life or change your world for the better. This is how the imagination works, and it is always working in a person's mind. Below is a diagram of the process:

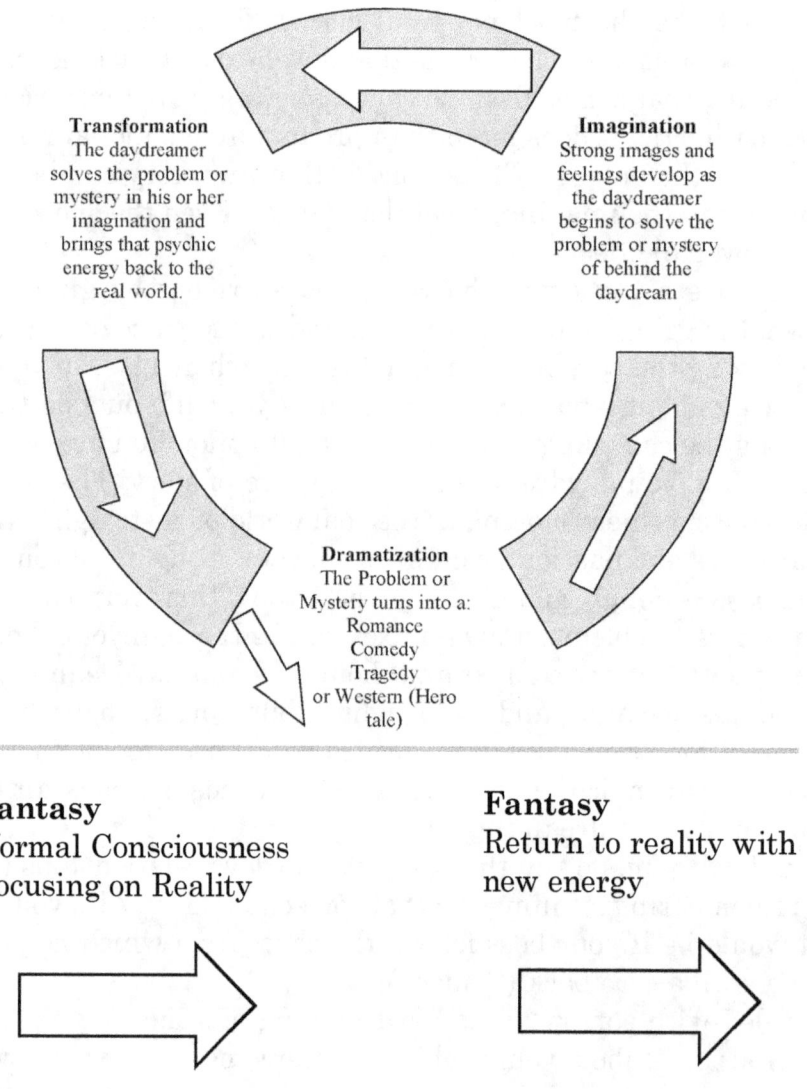

This process is exactly what a storyteller does for her listeners. She uses words inviting them to walk through their own imaginations. What is different is that the storyteller has a complete story. Our daydreams are not complete stories. If you think about the activity of daydreaming, what every person is trying to do is to finish the story, or make a wish come true that will finish the story.

For a story to be complete and meaningful, it only needs four elements or four pictures. These include: A Main Character or characters; a problem that is a mystery; a moment or image of magic; and an image that solves the mystery and transforms one of the characters. Let's look at these elements individually:

Characters

Celtic storytellers believed that the essence of a story lies in the characters of the story. They believed that each individual has three separate identities: the public self, the private self, and a secret self, or that place in the soul of the person where his innermost dreams lie dormant. People rarely share their secret selves with others. However, when they listen to a meaningful story, the soul of the listener, the secret self, is identifying with the main character and secretly asking, "Is that me? Could that be me? Is that going to be the story of my life?

The Problem/Mystery

Stories are all about solving problems and mysteries as they relate to the human condition. If there were no problems, then there would be no stories. When a loved one asks us, "How was your day?" They are inviting us to tell our stories. Most of us answer by saying something like, "It was going fine until . . . (This problem came along). For too many people, who do not feel they have any problems, or do not want to think about the challenges of their day, the response is simple, "My day was okay." Then he goes and turns on the television to watch the stories of people he does not know, people who are not real, people he does not love. He absorbs himself into stories of profane social fantasies and not personal dreams.

There are a lot of people who believe that their lives are boring and that they have no stories to tell. They have plenty of problems, but they're trivial and do not mean anything. It is vital for the storyteller to understand and articulate the problem in a story as not just a problem, but a problem that is also a mystery. When I get a flat tire, I have a problem. When I get a flat tire and I look up to the sky and scream "Why me God?" that's a problem that is also a mystery.

Magic

As important as the "who" or characters of most stories begin with are, a good story has magic in it. We live in a world of surprises. A world filled with irony and paradox. Strange happenings are everywhere. A day does not go by when we are asked . . . "Did you hear what happened?"

For some reason we tend to focus on the dark magic and often miss the positive magic. In the case of the flat tire, a stranger might come out of nowhere and fix the tire for me. Most magical moments in every great story can be found when a great paradox presents itself in the story. Once again, people do not think that their personal stories are any good because they do not have any magic in them. They think magic is something that literally happens and not something the imagination creates through metaphor, simile, and symbol. People do not think there are two basic truths in the world of story. The exact visible historical truth they see with their eyes, and the symbolic Truth that flows from their souls. When a good story is told, the listener passively hears the events of the story, but his soul actively experiences the symbolic meaning of that same story. You cannot get to the latter without the use of imagination and symbolism.

Character Transformation

The end result of every story is that the main character mentioned in the beginning is not the same person in the end of the story. The mystery has been resolved for better or for worse. Some stories transform the simple person into a hero, while other tragic stories transform the main character into a villain or tragic figure. The action of the main character going through his or her transformation can always be identified as a rite of passage. The secret self of the listener who personally identifies with the rite of passage that the main character of the story goes through is how the story touches the soul of the listener. Life is but a series of rites of passage. The human spirit is constantly trying to get through the symbolic gates of life—trying to actualize the soul of the human being.

Here is an explanation and a diagram explaining how the storyteller takes a listener through these four stages of a story.

Stage One

The listener starts listening to the story. He or she is focused on the teller.

Stage Two

The listener hears the introduction and the opening description of the characters.

Stage Three

The listener hears the problem/mystery of the main character. In many stories, there is more than one problem. When they collide is when the crisis of the story begins setting the stage for the magic to present itself. The listener unconsciously begins to compare themselves to the main character and his or her mystery. The Secret self, or deep inner self of the listener, is asking questions like, "Is that me? Could I be like that? Is that how I feel in this particular situation?"

Stage Four

The magic moment comes where the mystery is solved. The listener who has psychologically walked through the story as a symbolic main character receives an insight about his or her life that touches the soul.

Stage Five

With the resolution to the mystery, the identity of the main character or characters is not the same. For better or for worse, they are not the same person that they were before. A transformation has taken place. The listener has received an image of what it is like to walk through the rite of passage that the main character of the story passed through.

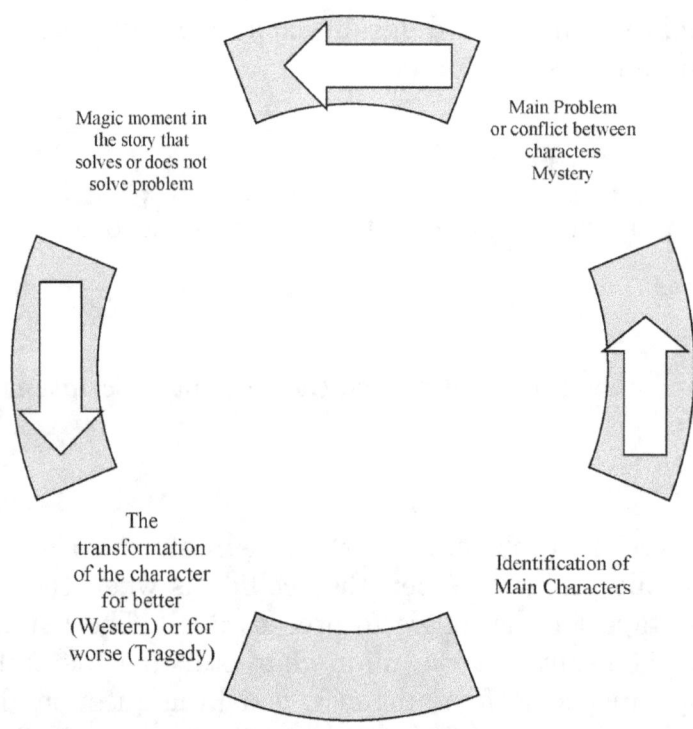

EXERCISE

Read the story of **The Boatman** and identify the four elements of a story through the pictures created by the words.

THE BOATMAN

A scholar asked a boatman to row him across a river. The journey to the other shore was long and slow. Before they reached midway, the scholar grew bored and began a conversation.

"Boatman," he called out, "let us pass the time by speaking of interesting matters. Have you ever studied phonetics and grammar?"

"No," replied the boatman, "I have no use for those tools."

"What a pity," snickered the scholar. "You have wasted half of your life! It is useful to know those rules."

Suddenly, the boat struck a sharp rock in the middle of the river and began to fill with water. The boatman turned to the scholar and said, "Pardon my humble mind, which appears to you so dim. Wise man, tell me, have you ever learned to swim?"

"No!" scoffed the scholar. "I have immersed myself in thinking."

"In that case," said the boatman, "you have wasted all your life. Alas, the boat is sinking."

ANALYSIS

Who are the characters of the story?
The main characters are the boatman and the scholar.

What are the major problems or mystery behind the story?
The scholar needs to cross the river.
The journey is a long one.
The boatman does not know or have use for the rules of phonetics and grammar, and this makes the scholar believe that the boatman has wasted half his life.

The mystery:
The scholar is wondering how a person could have no use for phonetics and grammar in his life. Another mystery is the boat crossing the river.

What is the magical moment of the story?
What novel or imaginational moment occurs in the story?
What image touches the soul of the listener?
When the boat strikes the sharp rock and turns the tables on the scholar.

How are the characters transformed?
The boatman becomes the wise one, and the scholar is seen as a fool.

EXERCISE

When the storyteller tells a story, she has three basic goals in which she wants to engage her listeners. These goals are invitation, wonder, and meaning. The teller wants to invite the listener into her world of story. She wants to engage the souls of her listeners by creating mystery and wonder, and finally, she wants to teach a lesson or a meaningful truth to her listeners.

In putting together a story, many tellers and the writer start with the lesson they are trying to teach. Once this is established, the other parts of the story fall into place. When a young person is struggling to solve a problem in her life, the mentor/storyteller does not act like the world's greatest expert and tell her what to do. He is reminded of a lesson he learned from a similar experience. With that lesson in mind, he simply tells the story of his experience with that lesson guiding his tell. The young person can now learn and solve the problem for herself.

My experience in storytelling and writing is that the lesson or moral of the story presents itself when two major images or symbols of the story collide, or sometimes, kiss. The message of the story is the result of the collision or kiss.

For example, the message of the Boatman story might be: **humility always beats out arrogance**. The image of humility is the picture of the boatman, while the image of arrogance is the scholar. The last image of the story is the scholar stranded on the sinking boat. The value of being humble is seen as the scholar stands in the sinking ship.

Using the message of how life can be a humbling experience, create your own wisdom statement and develop a story. Take a personal experience, add a little imagination and symbol to it, and develop it into a version of a common human experience

Some examples might include:

Write the story about the know-it-all family member, who refuses to take advice. The pride of a man refusing to stop and ask directions is very common.

A story from adolescence or that time in life when we are all "too big for our britches."

A story, where no one believes what a child has said and it turns out to be the truth.

A story, where no one believes what an elder has said and it turns out to be the truth.

Making the Pictures Talk: Learning and Remembering Stories

When people start out telling stories, they try to memorize them word for word and soon become discouraged. Stories are not meant for memorization. In fact, Anne Pellowski, one of the leading scholars on storytelling, does not believe a story is a real story unless something spontaneous or unplanned happens between the teller and audience. No two tellers ever tale the same story the same way, and no two listeners ever hear the same story.

While a teller is telling a story, his mind is taking a series of pictures in his head, translating them into words. The listener hears the words and retranslates them into his own mind, adding a personal touch to the story by using his own imagination. What is vital is that the storyteller is able to go to a place in her mind where she feels comfortable so that they can see what they need to communicate and simply act as a medium for communicating it.

Imagine that you are going to describe to me the living room of your house. In your mind, you will go to your living room. You will feel quite comfortable describing the room because you have been there so many times. When it comes to being specific, you will not tell me about every piece in the room. You will tell me just enough to get a good idea of what the room looks like. However, of all the things in the room that you describe, you will probably pick the objects that you think will most interest me. You may describe a certain picture to me but leave it out when you describe the room to someone else. Why? Because we interact with each audience differently.

The practice of learning a story is the same as describing things in a room that you have been in many times before. If you can communicate images of each of the four elements of the story, then you have a legitimate story. How you describe the specific images naturally flows from your imagination and the relationship you have with the audience. Creating in your mind the four basic images is like sitting down in a room you have been to several times before. Next, all you have to do is figure out the most relevant objects in the room to describe before moving on to the next room to describe the next set of objects. It is the same way in telling a simple story. The storyteller simply goes to a scene in the story and articulates all the characters, objects, and actions in that scene. The teller sequentially goes through each of the four scenes that have the characters, the problem/mystery, the image of magic, and the image of transformation.

Most of the formal stories that we want to tell, personal or traditional, cannot totally be performed off the top of our head. We have to do some memorizing. Of all the formulas presented, the best that I have heard is to memorize the introduction and conclusion of the story and then outline the story in pictures developing what storytellers call a storyboard. By storyboarding a story, I mean that you actually draw out the images of the story in the sequence of a storyboard in the same way that a comic book is designed. You do not have to be an artist to do this! You can draw stick images.

You simply draw a different cell for each time the location of the characters changes or when there is a complete scene changing in the activity of those characters.

The first thing to do after putting the story on a storyboard is to identify the four images that project the basic images of the story into your imagination. All other descriptors (pictures or cells) enhance the story. You can add features as you wish or are inspired. With this, you have set the major ideas that make the tale a complete story. Notice how you can divide the scenes into four basic pictures. Next, you look at the pictures while verbalizing the story. Do this several times and then verbalize the pictures without looking at them.

Below is an example of a storyboard helping me to learn the story "The Boatman."

THE BOATMAN

A scholar asked a boatman to row him across a river. The journey to the other shore was long and slow. Before they reached midway, the scholar grew bored and began a conversation.

"Boatman," he called out, "let us pass the time by speaking of interesting matters. Have you ever studied phonetics and grammar?"

"No," replied the boatman, "I have no use for those tools."

"What a pity," snickered the scholar. "You have wasted half of your life! It is useful to know those rules."

Suddenly, the boat struck a sharp rock in the middle of the river and began to fill with water. The boatman turned to the scholar and said, "Pardon my humble mind, which appears to you so dim. Wise man, tell me, have you ever learned to swim?"

"No!" scoffed the scholar. "I have immersed myself in thinking."

"In that case," said the boatman, "you have wasted all your life. Alas, the boat is sinking."

The Human Storyboard

Another way to take this technique to the next level is by creating a human storyboard. Get a bunch of friends or family members together and have each person become an element of each scene in your storyboard. Give them the characters to play and have them act out each cell of your storyboard. Yes, people need to assume the roles of inanimate objects found in the story. It makes the exercise great fun for everyone. Become like the director who is organizing or blocking each scene of a movie. Give each person direction and the dialogue that you want them to use. When there is a movement of a character in a scene, you have the character move while standing in place. As for the speed of the movement, you might want to ask the person to pantomime moving in slow motion. It will allow the entire image to stick into your memory. Have the performers act out each individual cell of your storyboard. After you have them performing what you want to see, then freeze that frame in your mind and go on to the next cell. In using this technique, the story is no longer a series of pictures on a page; it is actually something that you have literally experienced.

The Guaranteed Way to Remember a Story

If an individual has a "why" to tell a story, then she will always find a way to remember it and tell it. The simplest of stories are filled with the greatest amounts of truth and wisdom. Wisdom is one of the few gifts of infinite value that we do not have to pay for. It is priceless—minus the credit card. If you read or hear a story that touches your heart, the thing to do is to tell it to other people. Tell it and tell it again. The first few times, you will stumble. By the third time, you will be able to get to the four major images in the proper order. By the fifth or sixth time, you will have the story down. By the tenth telling, you will be able to make adjustments to the story while telling it to meet the different needs of the audience. This is the power of storytelling.

Telling Stories in Ways that Inspire, Sing and Dance

Sitting down and learning a story takes a great deal more time than simply reading the story out loud, but the payoff is much greater. Telling a story off text allows the teller to look into the eyes of the listener. It's like the old English saying, "The eyes are windows to the soul." There is nothing more powerful than seeing the light in the eyes of a listener whose soul has been touched by a story. Powerful words have a magic of their own when entering the minds of the listeners.

In general, the storyteller is the narrator of the story, but with a minimal amount of effort and a good sense of play, that same storyteller can become every character, every object, and every sound in that story. This brings energy to the story that can make the soul dance. The four techniques that bring stories to life include establishing an intimate relationship with the audience, the use of kinesthetic (body movement), characterization, and the use of sound and music.

Audience Relationship

The job of the storyteller is not to seem larger than life like the actor dressed up as Don Quixote on the Broadway stage. Intimacy is the main goal of the relationship between the audience and the teller. The best storytellers are those who can establish an intimate relationship with the audience. They create an atmosphere that is as if everyone is sitting on a front porch, drinking lemonade. Some storytellers establish this relationship by simply opening their story with a nice conversation. My own style is to ask the audience questions about their day, who they are, and how their lives are going. I tell them a little bit about me, and I always include something novel and out of the ordinary. Examples would include how many brothers and sisters I have (six) or asking the audience to guess what sport I was an All-American in during my youth. Any information that develops a give-and-take between the audience and me brings us closer together and produces an intimate setting.

I think it is a good practice to take the lesson of the story and turn it into some type of question to ask the audience before the story. I often ask the audience questions about elitism and arrogance in America before I tell "The Boatman" story. Another tool that I use is to ask the audience questions that directly relate to the major image or metaphor of the story. For me, the major image of "The Boatman" story is two men in a sinking ship. The metaphor serves as a basis for my opening questions. Examples would include the following:

1. "Has anyone every literally or figuratively been in a sinking ship?"
2. "Does anyone feel that our society or the world we live in is like a sinking ship?"

As the audience answers these questions, the intimacy begins to flow, and it builds up anticipation for the telling of the story.

Kinesthetic or Body Movement of the Story

At the heart of storytelling is play. When you tell stories, you play with ideas, images, and truths. The creative use of sarcasm can bring humor to a story while a strong metaphor brings wonder. When the storyteller gives himself or herself permission to let the words play through his or her body, it creates a new way for the listener to hear the story and see the world.

The best place for a storyteller to learn how to get their whole body into the act is while performing for children. The kids love slapstick humor of all kinds. They love to see the faces of the monkey and hear the lion's roar. They like their storytellers to be a little bit weird. Once the storyteller gives herself permission to play, then being a little bit weird can be a lot of fun.

When we talk about blocking a story in the way that the steps of a play are acted out, then we are looking at storytelling as a form of theater—or what I call "theatrical storytelling." The best technique is for the storyteller to record herself telling the story on compact disc or cassette tape. The storyteller can go through the tape and get a visual image of how each character and object moves throughout the story. The teller does not have to add all of them to the story, just a few to put an accent on it.

EXERCISE

Go back and reread "The Boatman" story. As you read it, visualize the motions of the people and the objects throughout the story. Listed below are examples of what I see when I try to block the story:

1. I see a very small old boat.
2. I see the scholar standing with his nose up in the air.
3. I see the scholar as a small man who walks and moves his body as if he were a very tall man.
4. I see the scholar dressed elegantly.
5. I see the boatman as taller than the scholar but always bent down in humility.
6. I see the boat going up and down, lapping against the water.

7. I see that boat hit the rock.
8. I see the water rushing into the boat, and the scholar does not even notice.
9. I see the boat sinking and the face of the scholar as it goes down.
10. I can see the boatman smiling and diving off the boat into the water.

Of the images listed above, I can use my body to pantomime or act out as I tell the story. I never use all of them. It would make the story too long. I pick one or two, and I change which ones I use, depending on my audience.

Characterization

Characterization is not the same as impersonation. You do not have to be this actor who can mimic the voice and act out the behaviors of famous people. Giving a character in your story a certain voice and behavioral presence almost always flows from the fun that you are having when telling the story. It is best to start with the personality of your characters when developing them. The lion has a roar. However, if the audience does not hear the roar of the lion in connection to its personality, then the audience will hear the sound, but they will not connect with it. The roar must flow from a defined personality of the character. If the audience hears the roar of a mean lion, they will have a deeper experience of the character and the roar itself. Once the character has a personality (shy, foolish, neurotic), the storyteller will be surprised at how little he has to do to make the character believable.

The best place to find the personalities of characters is from your own life. In the case of a mean lion, let the personality of the lion flow from someone you have dealt with in the real world who is truly mean. In this sense, it won't be a matter of telling yourself, "Okay, it's a mean lion. Now, what might a mean lion do or say?" You say to yourself, "Okay, the mean lion is my always angry Uncle." In this situation, you know exactly what my Uncle would say and how he would say it. The two would connect immediately from the image you have in your memory.

Central to characterization in the art of storytelling is how you use your face. Storytelling has been called "the theater of the face." When storytellers are videotaped, they are astounded at how much their face is telling the story as they speak the words. This is why simply reading a story cannot even be compared with the formal telling of a story. Developing characterization with the face is a very natural thing. Telling the story a few times in front of a mirror can allow you to develop an accent to make use of the face even more.

A lot of people will say to this direction: "But what if it makes me look silly?" The bottom line is that storytelling is about play. If you were sitting around the Thanksgiving dinner table, mimicking the way your brother used to cry when he was a kid, you would have no problems scrunching up your face. It is no different in front of an audience with which you have established some level of intimacy. Getting your face into the act is essential. In most cases, the teller simply has to give his or her face permission to be excited about the story, and the face will put on a wonderful performance without much coaching.

Developing the characterization in your storytelling is just a simple extension that the teller feels in terms of being comfortable with the audience. The teller turns into other people in his or her stories in relation to the intimacy he or she has with the audience. It happens naturally, and it grows with each telling of the story. The important thing is for the storyteller to start telling stories and keep telling stories, fostering confidence and intimacy with her audience.

EXERCISE

Choose a person in your life that has an animated personality or stands out as a real character. Then act out the behaviors below, emphasizing the unique way that you imagine each individual performing the behavior.

1. Act out the way that person laughs.
2. Act out how the person might sneeze.
3. Act out the way the person walks. Walk around a room for several minutes as that person.
4. Act out the way the person might eat a steak and drink a glass of wine.
5. Imitate the most prominent part of the person's character. Demonstrate his or her smile. Animate the way that he or she might speak. Simply become the person and animate his or her experiences. Capture his or her spirit and animate the behavior that symbolizes that spirit.

The list can go on and on. The central point is to find that personality trait that best fits the character and disposition of that character in the given story you are telling.

Music

Another powerful technique used in storytelling performance is music. We all want to try to make our stories dance a little bit. Music actually starts with a simple sound. Every story is filled with sounds, and the storyteller's job is to bring them out and make the story musical.

EXERCISE

Reread "The Boatman" story and identify every image that can also be heard as a sound. Listed below are the ones that I came up with:

1. The arrogance in the voice of the scholar.
2. The humility in the voice of the boatman.

3. The sound of the scholar stepping onto the boat.
4. The sound of the water lapping against the boat as it moves forward.
5. The sound of the boat crashing into the rock.
6. The sound of water flooding into the boat.

Of the sounds listed above, I can use my voice to make sound effects or onomatopoeia as I tell the story. I never use all of them. It would make the story too long. I pick one or two, and I change which ones I use, depending on my audience.

Real Music

What if you cannot play a musical instrument? What if your voice is so bad that you cannot even sing in the shower? In my career, I have found many ways to make music without knowing how to play certain instruments. I have purchased all kinds of percussion toys. I have told stories while playing musical accompaniment on the tape/CD player. All stories have a basic rhythm to them. The traditional instrument used to keep the rhythm of a story going is some form of a drum. I often use a drum by drumming the most simple of rhythms when the characters in the story are moving from one place to another. When available, I give people in the audience some type of percussion instrument to drum with me during the specific transition scenes. It is a very simple yet powerful technique.

I have also realized something about singing. Everyone can do it! Everyone can do it, especially if they do it while in character. If the character in the story is a bad singer, it has no reflection on the storyteller. You can announce to the audience how poorly the character sings before you do it. The audience appreciates the humor and the rhythm that the tune gives to the story. They accept the voice because it highlights a certain trait of the character in the story and not the person telling the story. What audiences respond to is the energy of the song.

Every storyteller also has the ability to create his or her own songs for an audience. It is as simple as the teller asking himself/herself how a given character might be defined if turned into a song or what song that character would sing over and over again. It only takes a phrase or two to count as a song. In a story I called "How the Skunk Got His Stripe," I characterize how mean the skunk is to the blackbird and the turtle by turning the way he makes fun of them into a simple song.

> Blackbird, blackbird, coat dark as night
> Ugliest thing within my sight
> Turtle, turtle with your cracked shell,
> Not only are you ugly, but you really smell

It is only a single verse, but small children (of all ages) love to hear about things that smell.

Why Stories Touch the Soul

Every year, I perform a storytelling show for students who are taking a course in Scripture. I give them a glimpse as to how the biblical stories were originally communicated through an oral as opposed to a written tradition. Before I start the show, I ask them to add up and multiply how many free hours they have during the summer. The actual number for those who do not have summer jobs is 1,440 hours. Then I ask them this: "Of all the hours you are free, how many hours are you bored?" The answer is always more than eight hundred.

I act like I am in shock, and I say, "There are over 250 TV stations you can watch. There are thousands of video games you can play. You have amusement parks, water parks, laser tag, skateboard parks, and even cosmic bowling. Even with all of this stimulation, how can you still be bored more than one-half of the time?"

I never get an answer. I then tell them that all that stuff meets the needs of your psyche, but none of it meets the needs of your soul. Stories are food for the souls, especially stories of spirit. I invite them to start reading the stories in Scripture. For me, reading the stories of Scripture is a constant struggle—a spiritual wrestling match. As I read the Scripture, my soul is always trying to put together the mystery of who God really is. I am asking God the age-old question, "Who are you?" I then read the Scriptures, and I reflect on my life, only to realize that through the sacred stories, God is asking me the same question. "Joe, Who are you?" More than on one occasion, like the story of Jacob wrestling with God and the next day becoming a whole new person with the new name of Israel, I have gained insight into my own personal story and walked into a whole new life.

I explain to the students that, more than any of those fun activities, their souls hunger for meaningful stories. I then proceed to perform my scriptural stories, and it never fails. Weeks, months, years later when I encounter some of the students who were in the audience that day, they always remember the stories.

What makes a good storyteller a great storyteller is that he or she knows stories speak directly to the secret self or soul of the listener. Every story starts and remains focused on the transformation of a main character. When a storyteller establishes a main character of a story, the soul of the listener is spiritually engaging with the identity of the main character. Stories can serve as mirrors illuminating the soul of the listener. The old stories work just as well as the new ones. Some call it the "luck of the Irish" when a friend seems to get all the breaks. Others believe that real magic is working in the friend's life in the same way that Athena helped Odysseus. From Narcissus to Elmo, people need to hear as many stories as possible in order to find a combination of characters or "whos" that authenticate their own true character.

The secret self of a human being is that place within where his or her soul lives. It is that inner dialogue whereby an individual tries to connect all the different identities she has into a composite self. The self is always in search of itself and meaning. It finds reflection of itself and meaning through story. This is why the human soul is always hungry for story. When a person speaks freely using the language of story, they become the center of the world to those who listen. The image often used to express this idea is the dropping of a stone in calm waters, causing a ripple effect.

Imagine that you are standing on a pier surrounded by a lake. You look down at the water, and it is completely still. It is not moving at all. In your hand is a small pebble. You take the pebble, hold it up in the air, and then drop it into the water. What do you see? You see ripples. The image of concentric circles was the archetype Confucius used to describe the different identities that a person develops in life. Each identity has a function to serve society and thus fulfill one's purpose in life. Below is a diagram of the image.

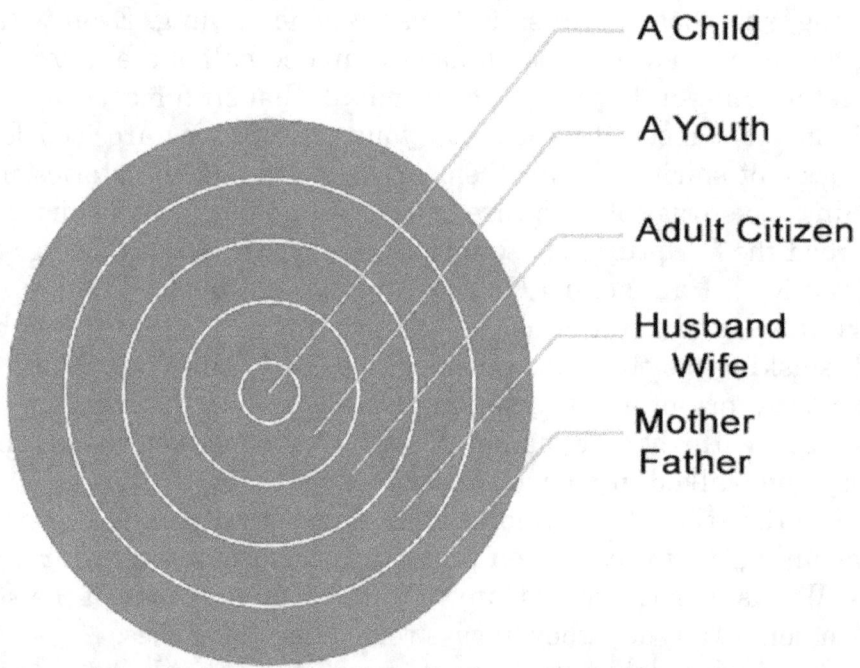

Now imagine you yourself as being the stone and that God from the heavens, or the gods of the sky, or the Fates from somewhere in outer space have dropped you into the Lake of Life. Carrying out the metaphor of being a stone dropped into a lake, where are you in the grand scheme of things? You must exist at the bottom of the lake. This is a metaphor representing us all trying to wade through the muddy waters of life. We are trying to keep our bodies and our minds up to the task of living a healthy, joyful, and meaningful life. It is easy for us to identify that we are scrounging through life like we are stuck at the bottom of the lake, but where are the ripples we bring to life? They exist at the top of the water. This can be seen as the second part of the metaphor. Every day each of us lives at the bottom of life's dirty lake. We are struggling to get through the mud of daily life. We are trying to wake ourselves up enough and get out of bed, trying to get our teeth brushed and our hair washed and trying to pay all our bills on time. At the same time, we are an energy influencing other people in ways that we cannot imagine. For every action, there is an equal and opposite reaction. The best way to see the ripples from the dirt is through story.

When a person tells a story, they exist on two planes—the lower and the upper. Storytelling is the act of helping others become conscious of the upper plane. A well-told story includes one identity from the past and another of the present. It demonstrates how people are transformed, and it gives the listener direction and affirmation as he chooses his own path in life. To the listener lost in the muck of life, it gives solace. To the listener with no direction and scared about the future, it gives hope.

The human person only has to reflect or symbolically look up to the reflection of the energy her presence brings to the world, but the only way to understand it is to tell the story of how it came to be. There are so many things about our lives that we do not understand until we verbalize them to another human being. Through the gift of telling our stories, we can see how our actions dramatically affect the lives of others for better or for worse. Our bodies are at the bottom of the lake, but our souls are creating energy, which is visible across the entire lake.

Extending the metaphor of our lives having a ripple effect in the world and the life stories of those around us, I identify each circle as one of the many identities each person has in his or her life. We are teachers, mothers, fathers, daughters, sons and a whole lot of other people within the context of our lives. Like the ripples, each identity is filled with all kinds of episodes of life. It is like riding around on a carousel.

EXERCISE

The purpose of this exercise is to take a look at the many identities you have assumed and continue to assume in life and to recall the experiences (the stories) that affirmed and transformed them. The basic element of every story is that, for better or for worse, the main character is not the same person at the end of the story that they were in the beginning. The character goes through a symbolic rite of passage and is transformed. A keyword is "symbolic."

More often than not, when people start to review their lives, one of the first things they have to say is "Nothing great has ever happened in my life. I never won the lottery. I never fought in a war. I was never on a championship team" and on and on. With just a little searching, every person can find a particular moment that was pregnant with symbolism. This is where the magic of all stories can be found. When it comes to a life of the soul, people cannot think literally; they must think more metaphorically and symbolically. Stories are going after the Truth with the capital *T* and not the literal truth.

In the final analysis, all the stories that I tell about myself and my life are true, and some of them actually happened. Below is a list of identities all of us have had at one point in our lives. I believe the average adult could come up with as many as fifty of them on his or her own—that's fifty stories!

Recall your personal character of the identities that you have lived through as identified in the list below, then seek out a specific experience at that stage of your life that transformed you. Find the experience and the symbol of that experience that called you to shed an identity and take on a new one.

Personal Identities: Story Starters

1. Toddler stories (Did anyone ever tell you your birth story?)
2. The story of how you got your name
3. Kindergarten to grammar school stories
4. Bike rider—from training wheels to the two wheels
5. Athlete stories—first base hit, first free throw, etc.
6. Cub Scout and Girl Scout episodes
7. Grammar school tales—detention, tests scores, etc.
8. Adolescent stories—first kiss, exposure to alcohol, drugs, getting a driver's license
9. Young adult stories—first job, traveling, getting married, paying one's own way
10. Adult stories—death of parents and friends, raising children (mother and father)

It is important, when searching out a story, to focus on the specific event that led to the powerful emotion in the story or the specific reason as to why you remember this story from all the others. The emotion and energy found in stories flow from images of raw passion, irony, paradox, and humor. Below are some story starters that focus on very specific yet common human experiences.

Other Story Prompts

Recalling a single image of a person's life can bring powerful feelings that call for a complete story to be told. Listed below are some story starters with such power:

1. Can you remember a pet that you once had that you do not have anymore?
2. Can you remember a time that you tried to cook something and it didn't turn out well?
3. Can you remember a time that you got in trouble for doing something that you had already been told not to do?
4. Can you remember a time when you broke something that belonged to someone else?
5. Can you remember a trip that you would not want to take again?
6. Can you remember a party or a date that you did not want to go on?
7. Can you remember a night that your parents never found out about?
8. Can you remember a time when you got sick at a very inconvenient moment?
9. Can you remember a birthday or a holiday that you would like (not like) to live over again?
10. Can you remember a time when you got lost or separated from your companion(s)?
11. Can you remember a time when you got locked out of where you needed to be?
12. Can you remember a time when you totally forgot an important date or appointment?
13. Can you remember a time when your first impression of someone turned out to be totally wrong?
14. Can you remember a time when you learned something from a child?
15. Can you remember a problem with a haircut? Makeup? Article of clothing?
16. Can you remember a time when you received a gift or a compliment that you did not deserve?
17. Can you remember a time when you almost won but not quite?
18. Can you remember a time when you were tricked by a person or got payback for someone who lied to you?

Bringing Meaning to Your Stories

Most people who talk to me about telling stories to others often claim to have little snippets of stories or anecdotes but never a full and complete story with a meaningful message. This is one of the main reasons why people tell me that they are not good storytellers.

When does a story have meaning? How can a person take a simple event from life and generate it into a complete and meaningful story? The answer to these questions lies in the desire for the storyteller to adventure from the literal to the symbolic. The teller must expand the image of a specific event and, like a balloon, blow it up, creating space for the listeners to identify with and wonder about that specific event.

As was mentioned in the poem "Naked Truth and Parable," the characters of the story must be expounded upon. Caricature must be used to build up characters, metaphor, and simile.

> Parable dressed Naked Truth in story's fine attire,
> with metaphor, poignant prose, and plots to inspire.
> With laughter and tears and adventure to unveil,
> together they went forth to spin a tale.

All stories have a critical moment right before the magic moment. In the critical moment before the imagination process begins, there is a dilemma that is connected to the identity of the major character. It is what some people call "the moment of truth." We find the meaning of a story by taking these two elements and turning them into symbols most often with the use of simile or metaphor. These two symbols are confronting each other, and something has to happen (magic) to bring them together as one. By taking the literal moment and making it symbolic, the story finds meaning. When the two symbols are creatively synthesized, a single metaphor develops, and that is usually the title of the story.

Here is an example: In 1989, I was on a mission trip to the Dominican Republic to work with the poor. The group I was with was riding on a bus going to the small village where we were going to work. As we passed a small village, a small child was standing on the edge of the road with a very swollen belly. A person on the bus looked at the boy and laughed out loud. He said, "Look at that kid. He has the biggest belly I have seen." We all started to smile when the leader of the trip told us that the child's belly was swollen because it did not have enough food in it. The child was actually starving.

That is the anecdote. Here is my story:

THE SWOLLEN BELLY

When we got off of the plane in the Santo Domingo, we could not have been more excited. Four adults and twelve high school students whose souls were filled to the brim with both excitement and fear about the journey we were about to take. A six-week mission of living with and working for the poorest people in the Dominican Republic.

Old John was the leader of the trip. He had worked with the people of the land for more than thirty years. His body looked old and tired, but every time he talked about his mission to the poor, you could see the fire in his eyes. Before we left the airport, he took us aside and spoke with us.

"Now, everybody, before we get in the van and travel, I need you to know that we are entering a new culture and, in many ways, a whole new world. It is vital to show respect to everyone you meet and help. These are a proud and honorable people. They are not going to be jumping up and down and saying thank you for every little bit of help you give. I truly believe that you are going to have a humble and meaningful experience, and I want to thank you beforehand."

We got into the van and drove for what seemed like days. The anticipation of where we were going and what we were going to experience kept us on full alert. At first, the houses we passed while driving down the long and winding roads were made of brick, but soon we only saw wooden shanties for homes, and finally, the only family homes we saw were straw huts. We were going deeper and deeper into this new world.

At one point, the van had to stop because a shepherd was guiding his flock across the road. It was then that one of the group members looked out the window and laughed. He was looking at a tiny boy standing by the side of the road with the skinniest arms and legs but a bloated belly.

The group member laughed out loud and said, "Look! Have you ever seen such a small kid with such a big belly? I'll bet he's a real beer drinker. Quick! Get a camera. Let's get a picture of this."

In all our ignorance, we began to smile and laugh at the kid. It was then that Old John got up and told us that the boy's belly was so large because it was swollen. It was swollen from hunger. It was that large because the child was malnourished and dying of hunger.

The member who made the joke immediately asked the driver to stop because he wanted to get that kid some food. Old John told the driver not to. He then told us that we were going to see hundreds, maybe even thousands, of small kids in this situation. The van drove in silence for the next hour. We were all coming to the realization that we were, indeed, in a whole new world.

ANALYSIS

The major moment in the story is when the leader tells the group why the belly is actually swollen. The battling symbols can be identified in many ways, including wealth versus poverty, wealthy ignorance versus simple innocence, or going to help the helpless versus being unable to help them. If you can think of more than that, you have just proven your ability to make your own stories meaningful. If you take a single snapshot of the entire story, you would see that the swollen belly is the image that most stands out. From this image comes the title of the story "Fact vs. Fiction."

As you can see, the story is much longer than the anecdote. Where did the rest come from? A lot of it is fact, but some of it is poetic license that I took to make the story meaningful. Let's separate fact from fiction.

Fact

1. Twelve of us did go to the Dominican Republic.
2. We did land at the airport and take a long bus ride to the site.
3. The group member did see the child on the side of the road with the belly.
4. He did laugh at the child, and others laughed out of ignorance.
5. Someone explained why the belly was swollen.

Fiction

1. There was a group leader, but he was not an old man. I made him an old man and gave him a character because it just came to my head. What I was really doing is developing a specific "who" in the story. I could have just as easily characterized the member of the group who spoke out as a very arrogant individual, but it simply did not come to me. Maybe that is the way that you would work it. As you begin to develop your own stories, this process becomes natural and almost automatic.

2. The group did get a speech about the new experience, but I cannot remember when it happened or what was actually said.
3. The member of the group who laughed at the swollen belly did not ask for a camera.
4. The leader did not say that we will see thousands of these kids.
5. The group member did not ask for the bus to be stopped.
6. The bus did not remain silent for an hour after the incident.

Note: All these fictional images came to me once I established the two conflicting symbols or metaphors. Every added image flows from metaphors and similes related to "ignorant but well-meaning wealth" contrasted against a stark image of "real poverty."

Our stories (and in effect, our lives) become literal symbols in the same way Christ is fully human and, at the same time, fully divine. I was an adult on the mission trip to the Dominican Republic, but spiritually, I was also a child. I really thought that, by sacrificing my summer to help the poor, I was performing an act of godly proportions. I was really excited to symbolically have the power of the love of God to bring to these people. When I encountered the child with the swollen belly, I saw the most human of images. I was trapped between the human and the divine. I was literally and symbolically caught in the mystery of Christ. The experience touched my soul, and that is why I need to tell this story.

Going from a Simple Story to a Complete Saga

Until this point, we have only dealt with telling meaningful short stories. However, all of us have had to sit through someone telling a story that went on and on, driving the listeners crazy. It's the old "I want to share with you how I became so successful at what I do. It all started when I was in my mother's womb . . ." Then the teller proceeds to share with all kinds of irrelevant (meaningless to the rest of his story) anecdotes.

Telling the longer story is the process by which the teller knits together a series of smaller stories into a format that connects the stories with a single larger tale. When it comes to telling a biography, a full folktale, or a myth, there are seven key elements instead of four I have previously described. The teller's job is to go from one element to the next while dispersing episodes in between. Master storyteller Jim May identifies the seven elements as follows:

1. A main character
2. A problem for the main character
3. A mentor
4. A magical gift
5. A crisis and testing of character's spirit
6. A resolution to the testing
7. A ritual ending

A Main Character

It is, at this point, where you tell a small story about who the character is and what experiences or story most made him or her that way. It is not just a description of a person; it is a story of an experience that molded that person's character. If you take a closer look at all hero stories, the main character starts out as being orphaned in some manner—e.g., Batman, Superman, Spiderman, and Luke Skywalker.

A Problem

As has been mentioned before, all stories center on a problem that is also a mystery or a given series of problems. The quest of the main character in the story is to solve the problem. When the problem is resolved, the main character of the story has gone through a rite of passage, and he or she is transformed. He or she now has a new identity.

A Mentor

All great stories are guided by the presence or the voice of someone wise and mighty. It is the same with all great heroes and leaders. Every Luke Skywalker needs his Yoda. The term "mentor" is derived from a character in the *Odyssey*. When Odysseus left to fight in the Trojan War, he asked a friend by the name of Mentor to educate and direct the life of his son Telemachus. Mentor served as a helmsman on one of Odysseus' ships. The job of a helmsman is to keep the ship balanced, going in the right direction and following a direct course through the troubled waters of the sea. So it is in the story of every hero. Each hero needs a mentor to guide them.

Every person needs some type of mentor to become actualized. He or she needs to have some type of connection with the history of what has happened before him or her. He or she needs an agent who can help temper his or her passion. He or she needs someone to give him or her a roadmap on how to accomplish his or her dreams.

Magic (Special Gifts)

Every person has a special gift—a magic. Central to the theology of every major religion is that God gives each person a special gift to serve the greater cause of humanity and make a difference in the world. Each person needs to identify what their magic is and how to use it properly and wisely. It is the same in the process of every story.

The Testing of the Main Character (the Crisis)

This is the part of a story where the tension of the problem reaches its peak. The main character is forced into a situation where he or she must use his or her magic to solve the problem. Central to my idea of storytelling is to understand that, in all stories, the testing of the main character is the same as that character going through a rite of passage or a life passage. When telling a saga, the teller includes one major testing of the hero figure, as well as identifications of victories and failures in the character's past.

The Resolution

The next structural aspect of the story is the resolution. It is that moment when the crisis of the story is over. The universal images of a resolution in any story are a long, slow exhale or the "sigh of relief" or "breath of sorrow." If the hero properly used the magic that the mentor gave him or her, then the story is a Western or hero's tale. If the hero did not use the magic properly, then it is a tragedy.

The Ritual Ending

Every great story ends with a form of a ritual. Maybe the prince and princess get married. Maybe there is a big banquet or some other party including all the characters at the end of the story. When something great happens in our life, we celebrate it. From these celebrations, we develop rituals. Rituals are behaviors that affirm our personal and communal stories. The ritual is acknowledging the story has a meaning. A simple example would be the raising of a glass to honor a person who has completed a rite of passage, as is the tradition of the wedding toast.

An Application of the Longer Story

Whether writing or telling a long story, the first thing is to use the seven elements to make a complete story with as few descriptors as possible. You will later add single episodes into the story that parallel the major tale. A good example would be the story of Ray Romano in the ongoing saga of the show *Everybody Loves Raymond*. Because the show was going off the air, the writers wrote the last episode in a symbolic way that completed the entire saga. Here is the overall structure of the story of Ray Romano.

1. **Main character:** A husband and a father who does not want to grow up and take on adult responsibilities.
2. **Problem:** In every episode, Ray is confronted by a situation that asks him to act mature. He struggles, in a humorous way, to solve the problem. In trying to avoid the problem, he creates another problem. When the two problems collide, the crisis appears.
3. **Mentor:** With each episode, another member of the cast—his brother or father, sometimes his mother—gives Ray that bit of information that allows acting more mature and taking on his responsibilities.
4. **Magic:** Ray's magic is his humor. He always turns everything into a joke.
5. **Crisis:** With each episode, Ray is confronted, usually by his wife, that he must solve this problem of growing up and assuming responsibilities. The audience is laughing, but deep down, they are wondering why his wife does not divorce him.
6. **Resolution:** By the end of the episode, Ray has assumed his responsibility and now uses his humor in a way that everyone can enjoy—even his wife.
7. **Ritual ending:** If you were able to see the final episode, the last scene was the entire family sitting around a table, getting ready to have a meal together. Ray closes the episode by saying, "This is nice, real nice." The final image of the final show is of a family having a meal together.

Learning How to Perform the Longer Story

If you want to tell a long story or saga, you simply add the seven images as signposts in a longer storyboard. Within the one long storyboard are the small episodes that accent the larger storyboard. These episodes can be broken down to the four images mentioned earlier.

The result is that the storyteller has one big storyboard covering the process of the seven elements as they apply to the entire story. Within specific cells are smaller stories that can be outlined as a separate storyboard. An example would be giving the main character of a story a funny name and then telling the short story of how the character got that name.

When learning the story, the teller knows that they should not leave one cell of the storyboard until all the images within that cell and the smaller cell have been articulated. The storyteller keeps the story from getting too long or boring by always keeping in mind that the story must keep trying to get to the next cell, which identifies the next element of the story.

You may also want to put the story on tape and listen to it over and over. You do not memorize. Developing images in your mind, you visualize each cell. You then ask yourself, "Okay, describe what you see and what happens to the main character in the first cell of the storyboard." You next take that image and add the images of the stories problem or mystery and so on until you get to the ritual ending of the story.

Keep your mind in a signal cell until you identify enough descriptors that satisfy the needs of that cell. When you are comfortable and feel that the description of the cell is complete, move to the next cell of the storyboard.

You are not memorizing every word in each cell. You are simply describing what comes to your mind. The guaranteed way of learning the story is to tell and continue to tell the story to other people. Yes, you will have to stop at a cell and wait until you're ready to go on to another cell. Yes, you will have to return to cells when you realize that you forgot something. However, based on how the listener responds, there will be a natural editor at work inside you, putting the story together in as a complete piece. It happens naturally; it is the way that our minds and spirits are wired to work.

The Greatest Stories Never Told

*Tell it to your children, and your children to their children,
and their children to the next generation (Joel 1:3)*

As a professional storyteller, more than half of the shows that I perform are in nursing homes. I always show up with my guitar and my selection of stories that remind the listeners of times gone by when they were young. I make it a point to stay a while after the show and mingle with the elders. It never fails. I always leave with much better stories than I performed. The elders of these communities have the most amazing stories. They include the plight of immigrants, living in poverty, surviving wars, and the list goes on and on.

One day, an elder woman told me the most amazing story of how she survived the depression by dancing and singing the streets. It took a little cajoling, but I got her to sing a couple of songs. Her eyes lit up like a bright light. Her entire appearance changed. She finished singing her songs with a great big smile. She shared with me that she had forgotten how hard life was and remembered how much fun she had singing and dancing through it. When I asked how she could forget such a wonderful story, she nearly broke my heart by telling me that no one had ever asked her about her past before.

Of all things, this generation needs to sustain the quality of life and culture that we enjoy. The stories and wisdom of our elders top the list. The psychological issue that gnaws at the spirit of people getting ready to leave this world and move onto the next is the question of dignity. Does my life have meaning or not? The psyche of an elderly person is constantly struggling between dignity and despair. If they know that they have lived a dignified life, they can embrace the later years, but the only way to keep the belief that they have lived a life of dignity is to tell their stories and share their wisdom with the next generation.

You do not have to spend much time with an elder to know if these needs are being met. They are happy and feeling dignified when you listen to them review their lives and tell their stories. When their stories are not being heard, they are in a state of despair and constantly complaining about how much their withering body hurts.

How to Record and Perform the Story of an Elder

In this life, the only real taste of immortality a person can receive is through story. We do not know exactly where Abraham and Moses and Jesus are, but they are very much alive through the stories we have of them. Sitting down with an elder and learning folktales that they were taught and putting their story into a single saga is the same as immortalizing them. I encourage every person to sit down with a grandparent, great-aunt, or any elderly person who still has a story to tell and learn their story.

It may seem like a daunting task, but it is required if the culture is going to find the wisdom to survive. The first thing to do is to get a recording device, then apply the process that was demonstrated above. Get one single story with all seven elements and design it into a single story with several small episodes and folktales they tell placed within it. In most cases, even a small story can have a powerful message. It can also be very healing for the elder.

The big story can be defined and put together by helping the elder develop a life graph of his or her life. A Life Graph is when you take a piece of graph paper and have the individual graph the high and low points of his or her life. They place the years below the X-axis of the graph and then mark specific positive and negative events in their lives along the Y-axis of the graph. They identify the intensity of how good or bad each experience was by marking high (in the positive quadrant) or low (in the negative quadrant) along the Y-axis. The life graph I took for my mother is shown below as an example.

					First Child	Child #2, #3, #4 Child #5, #6, #7		First/Second Grandchild		Fifth Grandchild
			Met Husband	Married			Parish Nurse			
	Birth of sister	Army Captain Nursing Degree								
Birth										
1930	(1933)	(1951)			(1957)	(1958 thru 1966)	(1990)	(1997)		(2003)
				Death of Mother			Husband Ill		Husband Injured	
	Poverty WWII								Sister Dies	Twin brother Dies
Death of Father										

Identifying the Overall Story

Main Character
- *Identities:* daughter, sister, nurse, soldier, mother, Irish
- *Attributes:* a strong, determined, caring, nurturing, humorous, storyteller; religious

Problems
- Death of her father
- Death of her mother
- Having little money
- A husband who gets injured and then ill
- All the problems that come with having seven children

Magic
- The ability to tell stories
- The ability to make people laugh
- An amazing faith
- A person who prayed for miracles and, when they did not come, made them happen herself
- Highly intelligent and studious
- Have great self-discipline and determination

Crisis
- The death of her father (immediate poverty)
- The death of her mother
- The injury and illness of her husband
- Every crisis that a mother goes through with her kids
- Being a nurse during the war

Resolutions

- Overcoming poverty
- Never losing a chance to tell her children about the grandparents they never met
- Married for forty-eight years
- Playing with her grandchildren

Rituals

- Hosting family celebrations
- Telling her grandchildren stories and constantly encouraging them to dream
- Calling each of her children to share a recent accomplishment of one of her grandchildren
- Going to church
- Saying the rosary each day
- Calling each child to inform them about activity in the community and how other people they grew up with are doing
- Reading the obituaries (this is a humorous one)

After the graph is completed, you go back through it with the elder. This time, you have them identify things that were happening in the society around them during the specific stages of their life. Try to determine what was happening in the world during their lives. How do the themes of those historical times parallel with their individual stories? Comparing and contrasting these two elements generates a lot of insight and wisdom.

Finally, you interview them, asking them questions about specific episodes in their lives that relate to the development of their character. Ask them about the great problems or challenges in their lives, the magical things that happened in their lives, the great tests they faced in their lives, the resolutions, and so on.

Finding the central theme or meaning to the story of life can be very challenging. Keep seeing the symbols behind the events. Keep seeing how metaphors fight and kiss each other in the stories. If that doesn't work, then you need to go and do something really radical. Ask them. Ask them what living a human life has meant. When the elder feels comfortable, they are open and honest about most of the things few people in our daily lives have the courage to talk about. My experience has been that I have the short tales etched in my mind with one telling. It never fails. The situation always seems to present itself to share the story with someone I encounter in the coming week. When you return to perform the stories they tell or their complete story on living a human life, you will see the complete power of story. The smile on their face radiates eternity. Stories truly have the power to heal.

Starting and Maintaining a Family Storytelling Tradition

And the youngest child at the table asked, "Father, why is this night different from all other nights?" (Initiation of the Seder Meal)

The Seder meal is one of the most special celebrations in the Jewish calendar. It is a special dinner that commemorates the remembrance of the Passover. The tradition is to have the youngest child at the table ask the question above, and then the father or leader tells the entire story of how Moses led the Jews out of slavery. This ritual has connected Jewish families to their past for more than four thousand years. It is essential to the Jewish identity to keep telling this story over and over as the years go by.

Stories are central to every family retaining its unique identity. However, we are losing time and place to share these stories with our children. Traditionally, family storytelling occurred with the dessert after a family meal, like Thanksgiving. Today, most men eat their dessert in front of the television, watching the ball game, while the women devour the newspapers, looking for Christmas items on sale.

Young people are losing their sense of being connected to a family that has survived countless generations. Most kids I ask do not know what the word for their last name means in its original language. In my twenty years as a teacher and professional storytelling, I have discovered that our children are hungry, even starving, for stories. Whether it's a story about family immigration, a parent courtship tale, or even their very own birth story, our young people have a deep-rooted need to hear the stories from the past that have given them an identity in the present and have served as the path by which they are going to live out their own destiny.

Getting Everyone into the Act as a Family Tradition

The best place to start and renew a tradition of storytelling in your family is to acknowledge the ones you already have. Start with the Christmas ornaments. Every family keeps their ornaments, and as time goes on, each ornament reminds them an earlier Christmas. It is important to recognize the power of the symbolism in those ornaments. The goal of the storytelling tradition is to have stories being told with that kind of emotional power all the time. Here are some ideas to keep the stories flowing:

Family Meals

Families need to find time to have more family meals together. They need to find more family stories to tell at the dinner table. All meals are celebrations. All celebrations are centered in a story.

EXERCISE

In this exercise, the leaders or elders of a household sit down with a calendar and choose a single month to review. The group needs to take a look at each day of the single month on that character and come up with something to celebrate or commemorate for that day. The family needs to get together and take a long look at the calendar. If you think hard enough, each meal could be identified after some event connected to the lives of family members. Birthday stories can be celebrated; this includes immediate family members and extended family members, as well as pets and friends. With the acknowledgment of each person comes a story. Stories celebrating anniversaries could focus on anniversaries events that include marriage, broken bones, first kisses, and athletic feats, past vacations and journeys, and on and on. A father might sit down at the dinner table, pick up a glass, and say, "Today we celebrating the first time I kissed your mother." I guarantee that all the kids will be waiting to hear the tale.

When the event is identified, the storyteller simply takes the anecdote or event and turns it into a complete and meaningful story. The teller identifies the main characters, isolates the problem, finds the magic, and identifies the transformation of the main character in the story. The teller simply walks through the four images of developing a good story. Connecting two metaphors or symbolic images will give the story meaning. The teller can add a little nostalgia about the time and place the story occurred to give it some flavor.

Another activity is the game of "Bring a story, song, joke, or dance to the table, or you don't eat." The Irish were once known to make their children literally sing and dance for their supper. I started this tradition in my house by leaving joke books in every room. Dinner did not start until every person had told a joke. We have worked it up to telling complete stories before, during, and after our family meals.

Telling the Entire Family Saga

It was a tradition in nearly all families that one person was identified as the bearer of the family story. This person was the one that everyone seemed to open up to. This was the person who spent a great deal with his or her grandparents. It seems that fewer people are assuming this role, and much of the family oral history is being lost. Making the history something physical and visible is one way to keep the tales of the family experience going.

In the past, it was most effectively done by having a family quilt that was handed down through the generations. Each generation of women would sew new images onto the quilt that symbolized the latest experiences of the family. They may place a general image on the quilt surrounded by sequins. Each sequin would represent a specific episode in the lives of the family.

Like so many things, certain dispositions of the modern-day family may not be conducive to making an entire quilt, so I use a technique that has been used for generations among storytellers. I went out and purchased a fishing net. As time has gone by, I have attached to that net any small token which has reminded me of a family story. I have a diagram of the net below. Having that token or symbol representing the story teaches kids the importance of symbols. They become more powerful than family pictures because they project images and meanings that go beyond pictures and words. Every time I go into a gift shop, antique store, or dollar store, my entire spirit is scanning all the items looking for one thing that might symbolize an event in my life or lives of others in my family. It's amazing to see how our lives are so connected to the things around us in such a meaningful way.

Other ways of keeping a family storytelling tradition are as follows:

Opening up a family blog: An internet space where members of the families can go to and write down stories as they pertain to the history of the family is a blog. Members of the family could identify certain themes to write stories each year—things like stories of things that happened in the old house, stories of things that got broken while the kids were playing with them, and on and on. What is going to happen is that certain members of the family are going to remember certain events differently, and this will create an internet dialogue that will reveal different versions of the same stories. If each member of the family makes on a couple of entries each year, the blog becomes a very real and nostalgic look at the family through time.

Tape recording stories: By asking each person to record or tell one of the stories, you are retaining not only the story but also the voice of the teller. Once again, the stories can easily be recorded and organized through the computer.

Parenting Through Story

God only gives children to couples who know at least
one hundred stories. (Walibi proverb)

Could you imagine raising a child without ever having to raise your voice, scold, hit, or punish him? I know it seems inconceivable, but it's possible, and it's true. Professional storyteller Dovie Thomson was raised by her parents and grandparents through stories. Every time Dovie misbehaved, her Lakota mother or grandmother would sit her down and tell her a native story. The story would always have a character who, just like Dovie, was behaving inappropriately. Each story ended with the main character learning a new life lesson or reason for changing his or her behavior. By the third or fourth time Dovie demonstrated a particular inappropriate behavior, her parents or grandparents would have her tell the story back to them. Dovie was a rather rambunctious kid. She knew fifty-nine stories by heart before she was ten years old.

Finding simple stories for your children and telling them often has a great effect on their behavior and their understanding of right and wrong. Teaching your children through story, having them tell a story that parallels their misbehavior back to you, also has a much more powerful long-term effect than simply sending the child to his room for a timeout. Instead of scolding your child when misbehaving, I invite you to call them over, have them sit next to you, put your arms around them, and tell them a story. See if you get better results in bringing discipline to your children.

When it comes to setting your adolescents free into the real world, I feel it is imperative that each child know his or her family history regarding the challenges of those who have gone before her. If there is a history of mental illness, alcoholism, or drug addiction in the family, then the young person should be made aware of it. They need to hear not just the facts but also all the stories regarding the dangerous rites of passage they are going to encounter in their quest of becoming a mature and self-sufficient adult.

Information regarding the history of life choices is much more powerful and may remain on the minds of the young person when it is presented in the form of a complete story. The young person needs to hear the stories regarding the great successes of their family history, as well as the tales of family members who had made mistakes before them and brought a great deal amount of pain to those around them. Most of us want to tell stories to our teenagers with that moral message of "I am telling you this story so that you will not do this. I want you to learn from my mistakes." However, everyone knows the more you tell a teenager not to do something, the more he or she wants to try it. I strongly suggest that when you tell the dark stories of life to your children, do not focus on the message of right and wrong more than you focus on the emotional pain and sorrow that all the characters experienced in light of the tragedy. Remember that stories are about "who" and not "what." If the listener feels the sorrow of the victims in the story, they are more likely to think about it or recall it when placed in a situation that is similar to the one in the story.

Something interesting happens as parents chauffeur their children in the car from place to place. At around midlife, it seems that every little landmark on the road begins to remind them of their youth. Most people are frightened by it because they see it as a sign that they are getting old. People who try to block these impulses tend to go through what we now know as the "midlife crisis." They engage in all sorts of regressive behavior, trying to feel young again. The reality of the phenomenon is that the time has come for the parent to become an elder. It is a rite of passage where the spirit calls parents to share the stories of their lives and some of the things that they have learned. It takes some courage to turn down the radio or tell them to pull the earplugs of their iPods out. After riding the car of all the cacophony, you tell them your story. Will they listen? No. Will they remember it after you are gone? Every word of it! This is the magic of story.

There is also one more thing that adults can do for the social and emotional development of their children that is so radical that it will shock you. Read the story below.

THE KING'S MUSICIAN

Once upon a time, there were two brothers. Actually, they were the last two brothers of a family with seven brothers. They lived in Iceland. Now, don't mix Iceland up with Greenland. Greenland is the land that is full of ice while Iceland is the land that is mostly green. The father of the two boys owned a farm and, as was the tradition, would give each son a part of his land to raise his family when the time came. Well, when the time came for the last two brothers, there was no land left to give, so they had to make their own way in the world.

It wasn't long before the elder of the two brothers found an announcement from a king in a far-off land that he was holding auditions for new royal musicians. Both the brothers played several instruments, so the elder encouraged the younger brother to go with him. The problem was that the younger brother had just fallen in love. You know what love is? It consumes your soul and enfolds your entire being. The older brother told the younger brother that the only way he could be with his true love was to find a job. He could send for her when he raised enough money working for the king. So the younger brother promised his true love that they would be together forever soon and went with his elder brother.

The kingdom was far away. It was a long journey for the brothers, and by the time they got there for the auditions, it seemed that every musician in the world was there to try out. The younger brother's sorrow at being away from his true love was so great that he told his brother he did not want to play for the king. His brother said, "Stop talking about your sorrow and play it!"

The boy picked up a violin and played with a sadness that brought tears to the king's eyes. When asked to play another song, he picked up a trumpet and played all the love that was in his heart. Finally, he picked up a flute and played a soft, sweet melody with pictures of his future children being played to sleep in his mind.

Immediately the king stopped the auditions. He found the one musician he was looking for and would need no others. The younger brother was happy but heartbroken that he could not go back to his home with his elder brother. The brother promised and returned with the message that he would send for his true love as soon as he had enough money, but the elder brother, upon meeting the girl, soon realized why his younger brother loved this girl so much as he soon fell in love with her as well.

Just as the younger brother put enough money together to send for his true love, he had gotten word that his brother had married the girl that he loved more than life itself. He had been playing glorious music for the king and his court every night while thinking just of her. But on this night, there was not life, love, or hope in any note he played.

The court was disgruntled, and the king inquired, "My musician, what troubles you so that you cannot play so wonderfully as you have in the past?"

The young man just hunched his shoulders and let out a deep sigh.

"Why, surely there must be a problem. Problems are very rational things. They all have logical solutions. I listen to problems through my left ear, they dance in my brain, and I come up with very rational solutions. It is logical to see that I have not been rewarding you enough for your services. To the far east of my land are a cottage and a stable. I hereby grant that cottage to you."

The boy put his head down and played some more, but still, nothing beautiful came out. The court was disgruntled, and the king inquired, "My musician, what still troubles you that you cannot play so wonderfully as you have in the past?"

The young man just hunched his shoulders and let out a deep sigh.

"Why, surely there must be a problem. Problems are very rational things. They all have logical solutions. I listen to problems through my left ear, they dance in my brain, and I come up with very rational solutions. I tell you what. I will fill the stable next to the cottage with the finest of my horses."

When the lad did not play well again, the court became angry and defiant. Who was this young music maker to reject such wonderful gifts from the king and not play with his whole heart?

Immediately, the king dismissed everyone from the room except the young man. When they were gone, he got off his throne and walked directly to the lad. He said, "Son, I am the king of this land. Do you know why? It certainly isn't my good looks. I am the king of this land because I am the only person who knows that he has two ears. Through my left ear goes information that helps me solve logical problems, but the other ear—my right ear—goes directly to my heart and embraces illogical problems. Son, tell me your story, and I will listen to it with the ear that is connected to my heart."

So the musician told him his story. He told him of his one true love and how he had to leave her. Trying to fight back the tears, he told the king how his brother fell in love with the girl and married her. The king just listened. After a while, the young musician played a little bit. He came back the next day and cried some more but played a little bit longer and more beautiful than ever.

Well, the years went by. The young musician met a beautiful maiden from the kingdom, got married, and had a son of his own. It was the day after the musician saw his own son running through the fields of the kingdom hand in hand with a most beautiful young maiden. The boy was hunched over in a state of deep sorrow, walking up the way of the cottage. His father said, "Son, you look as if your best friend has died."

The boy shrugged his shoulders and stared at the ground.

The father said, "Why, surely there must be a problem. Problems are very rational things. They all have logical solutions. I listen to problems in my left ear, they dance in my brain, and I come up with very rational solutions. It is logical to see that you need more music in your life. Son, I have just made this new instrument, and you may have it."

The boy kept his head down and sighed some more.

The father said, "Son, I am the only musician in the king's court, and do you know why? It's certainly not my good looks. I am the only musician in the king's court because I am the only musician who knows he has two ears. My left ear is attached to my brain and allows me to solve problems logically. My right ear is attached to my heart and allows me to solve illogical problems. So tell me your story, and I will listen through the ear that is connected to my heart."

—A folktale retold by Sydney Lieberman

Conclusion

It is reasonable to say that storytelling is the oldest and original art form known to humanity. On one level, storytelling is the oldest of arts, yet from another level, it is always brand-new—as new and unique as each experience one person wants to share with another. Oftentimes, what makes a storytelling event successful is not the celebrated talent of the storyteller, but rather the intimacy a storyteller has with his audience. Inasmuch as stories are filled with irony and paradox, so are storytellers. They come in all shapes and sizes. When we try to categorize the storyteller as having a particular style, that same teller comes before a new audience and completely changes the way in which he or she tells a particular story. Why? Because the collective spirit of the audience asked him or her to. This is an interaction of life that cannot be experienced in any other medium. In the final analysis, we tell the stories we hear, and we become the stories we tell, but between the telling and the becoming, our own unique light shines on the world in a way that no light has ever shined before.

If every person is called to live a complete life, why not live it out as a work of art? Why not define life and our experience of it in the language of art, including hyperbole, metaphor, simile, poetry, and story. The one request of men and women most often made on their death beds is a request to be remembered. People dying often make the statement "Please remember me. Tell the children my story." Stories make life eternal. Bring eternity to your world by using the power of story.

"And they told stories happily ever after."

"I have come to believe that our younger generation is hungry for personal and meaningful stories. Whether it be ancestral immigration, parental courtship tales, or their very own birth stories, our children are starving for the stories that give their souls a sense of history from the past, their minds a sense of identity in the present, and their spirits a sense of vision as they venture forth to fulfill their dreams." (Joe Jekot)

"Research has revealed that the best predictor of the security of our children's attachment to us is our ability to narrate the story of our own life in a coherent fashion." (Daniel J. Siegel, MD, from his book *Mindsight: The New Science of Personal Transformation*)

Finding the Lost Art of Family Storytelling: A Guide for Parents, Grandparents, and Family Historians is a response to all the challenges for families raising kids in this generation. Experts tell us *what to do* in order to be the best we can be for our kids. Joe Jekot tells us *who to be*—ourselves. He is of the belief that storytelling is at the center of all aspects of family life and the formation of personal and communal identity. A good story told in the right way and at the right time can change the direction of a young person's life for the better. This guide empowers family storytellers to weave the tales that will allow young people to grow into purpose-driven and happy adults.

Joe teaches a simple four-step process by which a person can take any significant experience of life and transform it into a powerful story. The guide includes more than seventy story prompts and reflection questions that will draw out the hidden tales just waiting to be told.

Joe has a B.A. in theology and M.Ed. in community counseling from the Loyola University of Chicago. He is a certified *parent effectiveness trainer* and has completed a certificate in narrative healing. He is an active member of the National Storytelling Network, the Northlands Storytelling Network, and Illinois Storytelling Inc.

For more information on Joe's retreats, seminars, and performances, contact Joe at www.joejekot.com.

Bibliography

Bly, Robert, *Iron John*. New York: Vintage Books, 1992.

Davis, Donald, *Telling Your Own Stories*. Little Rock, Arkansas: August House Books, 1993.

Cameron, Julia, *The Artist's Way*. New York: Putnam Book, 1992.

Chinen, Allan, M.D., *Beyond the Hero*. New York: Putnam Book, 1993.

Estes, Clarissa, Ph.D., Women *Who Run with the Wolves*. New York: Random House Publishers, 1995.

Fausto-Sterling, Anne, *Myths of Gender*. New York: HarperCollins, 1992.

Forest, Heather, *Wisdom Tales from Around the World*. Little Rock, Arkansas: August House Books, 1996.

Forest, Heather, *Wonder Tales from Around the World*. Little Rock, Arkansas: August House Books, 1996.

Frankl, Victor, *Man's Search for Meaning: An Introduction to Logotherapy*. Boston, MA: Beacon Press, 1992 – 4th edition.

Hamilton, Edith, Mythology: *Timeless Tales of Gods and Heroes*, New York: Penguin Books, 1940.

Keen, Sam, & Valley-Fox, Anne, *Your Mythic Journey*. New York: Putnam Publishers, 1989.

Kendal, Haven, *Super Simple Storytelling*. Englewood, Colorado: Teachers Ideas Press, 2000.

Klinger, Eric, *Meaning and Void: Inner Experience and the Incentives of Peoples Lives*. Minneapolis, MN: University of Minnesota Press, 1977.

May, Jim, *The Farm on Nippersink Creek*. Little Rock, Arkansas: August House Publishers, 1994.

Meade, Michael, *Men and the water of Life*. Sanfrancisco: Harper Collins Publishers, 1993.

Merriam-Webster editors, *Webster's Dictionary of Word Origins*. New York: Barnes and Noble Books, 2004.

Spolin, Viola, *Improvisation for the Theater*. Evanston, Illinois: Northwestern University Press, 1999.

Tracy, David, *The Analogical Imagination: Christian Theology and a Culture of Pluralism.* New York: Crossroad Publishers, 1981.

Weisel, Elie, *Night.* New York: Bantam Books, 1982.

Ibid., *Souls on Fire.* New York: Random House, 1972.

Yalom, Irvin, *The Theory and Practice of Group Psychotherapy.* New York: Basic Books, 1995.

Tapes and Compact Discs

Bly, Robert, *Iron John and the Male Mode of Feeling.* Pacific Grove, CA: Oral Traditions Archives, 1991.

Heindlmayr Jackalene Crow, *Legends of the American Indians.* Florida: Celebrations Indians, Inc, 1997.

Hillman, James & Meade, Michael, *Character and Destiny: Authentic Threads in Life.* Pacific Grove, CA: Oral Traditions Archives, 1996.

Meade, Michael, *The Water of Life.* Boulder, CO: Sounds True Recordings, 1993.

Resources

Stories are everywhere, but I would like to list a few publishers who have made a firm commitment toward keeping all traditions of storytelling alive in and out of the classroom. The range of resources offered by these companies is complete.

To obtain catalogues with extensive offerings of books and tapes by and for storytellers, contact:

August House Publishers
P.O. Box 3223
Little Rock, AR 72203
Toll Free:800-284-8784
E-mail: order@augusthouse.com
Website: http://www.augusthouse.com

To Obtain more information about storytelling organizations, publications, and events, please contact

The National Storytelling Membership Association
116 ½ Weste main Street
Jonesborough, TN 37659
Toll-Free: 800-525-4514
Direct: 423-923-8201
Fax: 423-753-9331
E-mail: NSMA@naxs.net
Website: http://www.storynet.org

www.ingramcontent.com/pod-product-compliance
Lightning Source LLC
Chambersburg PA
CBHW081730100526
44591CB00016B/2568